# Straight Talk About...
# BULLYING

Jessica Pegis

Crabtree Publishing Company
www.crabtreebooks.com

Straight Talk About...

**Developed and produced by:** Netscribes Inc.

**Author:** Jessica Pegis

**Publishing plan research and development:**
Sean Charlebois, Reagan Miller
Crabtree Publishing Company

**Project Controller:** Sandeep Kumar G

**Editorial director:** Kathy Middleton

**Editors:** John Perritano, Molly Aloian

**Proofreader:** Kelly McNiven

**Art director:** Dibakar Acharjee

**Designer:** Shruti Aggarwal

**Cover design:** Margaret Amy Salter

**Production coordinator and
prepress technician:** Margaret Amy Salter

**Print coordinators:** Katherine Berti,
Margaret Amy Salter

**Consultant:** Susan Cooper, M.Ed.

**Photographs:**
Cover: iStockphoto/Thinkstock; Title page:
wavebreakmedia/Shutterstock Inc.; p.4:Pixel Memoirs/
Shutterstock Inc.; p.6:Anita Patterson Peppers/
Shutterstock Inc.; p.8:Netscribes Inc.; p.9:Netscribes
Inc.;p.10:GCRO Images/Shutterstock Inc.; p.12:Kamira/
Shutterstock Inc.; p.13:Vuk Vukmirovic/Shutterstock
Inc.; p.16:Sylvie Bouchard/Shutterstock Inc.; p.18:Tad
Denson/Shutterstock Inc.; p.21:oliveromg/Shutterstock
Inc.; p.22:Francis Wong Chee Yen/Shutterstock Inc.;
p.24:Peter Bernik/Shutterstock Inc.;p.25:Jose AS Reyes/
Shutterstock Inc.; p.26:Elena E/lisseeva/Shutterstock
Inc.; p.28:VBStock/istockphoto.com; p.29:Netscribes
Inc.;p.30:Low Chin Han:Shutterstock Inc.; p.32:
Gemenacom/Shutterstock Inc.; p.34:YURALAITS
ALBERT/Shutterstock Inc.; p.36:Galina Barskaya/
Shutterstock Inc.; p.37:Chris Pole/Shutterstock Inc.;
p.39:Monkey Business Images/Shutterstock inc.;
p.41:Feomarty Olga/Shutterstock Inc.; p.42:YanLev/
Shutterstock Inc.

**Library and Archives Canada Cataloguing in Publication**

Pegis, Jessica
      Bullying / Jessica Pegis.

(Straight talk about ...)

Includes index.
Issued in print and electronic formats.
ISBN 978-0-7787-2181-9 (bound).--ISBN 978-0-7787-2188-8 (pbk.).--
ISBN 978-1-4271-9064-2 (pdf).--ISBN 978-1-4271-9118-2 (html)

      1. Bullying--Juvenile literature.  I. Title.  II. Series: Straight talk
about-- (St. Catharines, Ont.)

BF637.B85P45 2013          j302.34'3          C2013-902670-3
                                              C2013-902671-1

**Library of Congress Cataloging-in-Publication Data**

CIP available at Library of Congress

# Crabtree Publishing Company

www.crabtreebooks.com          1-800-387-7650

Printed in the USA/052013/JA20130412

**Published in Canada**
**Crabtree Publishing**
616 Welland Ave.
St. Catharines, ON
L2M 5V6

**Published in the United States**
**Crabtree Publishing**
PMB 59051
350 Fifth Avenue, 59th Floor
New York, New York 10118

**Published in the United Kingdom**
**Crabtree Publishing**
Maritime House
Basin Road North, Hove
BN41 1WR

**Published in Australia**
**Crabtree Publishing**
3 Charles Street
Coburg North
VIC, 3058

Check Out Receipt

North Pulaski

Tuesday, December 12, 2017
1:50:45 PM

Item: R0440256310
Title: Bullying
Due: 01/02/2018

Item: R0446208399
Title: The war that saved my life
Due: 01/02/2018

Item: R0428224224
Title: Finding family
Due: 01/02/2018

Total items: 3

Thank You!

705

# CONTENTS

Arthur climbed the stairs to the third floor and took a deep breath, just in time for the worst 45 seconds of his day. This was the hallway he had to take to social studies class. It was the only class he had on the second floor, and he was always anxious by the time he got there. Arthur held his breath for a second and listened for voices.

Sure enough, Jason was there with his posse, Kyle and Liam. The three boys lounged against the lockers, hands in their pockets, as Arthur rounded the corner.

"Hey, Arthur," Jason drawled. "How's it goin'?"

*Keep walking, keep walking, don't stop walking,* Arthur thought to himself.

"Hey, you!" Kyle was on Arthur's back in a flash, whirling him around. "Are you freakin' deaf? You were asked a question. Now, answer."

"I-I'm fine," Arthur stammered. "I just need to get to class."

Jason stared at Arthur as though he were a worm on a hook. "Turn him around," Jason ordered Kyle. "Today's his lucky day cause he doesn't get smacked."

Jason removed a small water pistol from his pocket and took aim at Arthur's legs and crotch. It took Jason about ten seconds to empty the pistol while Kyle and Liam held Arthur still.

"There," said Jason, a huge grin spreading across his face. "You're done. Baby peed his pants. Too bad you forgot your pull-ups. Now get lost."

# Introduction
## A Bad Situation

Arthur has been bullied nonstop by Jason, Kyle, and Liam since the beginning of the seventh grade. Arthur has been punched, kicked, slapped, spat on—and now sprayed with a water pistol. He has been called "stupid," "a fag," and "unfit to live." Arthur just moved to town with his parents. He feels lost and lonely and is embarrassed to tell anyone about his situation.

Arthur is being bullied.

In this book, you will learn about different types of bullying, why people bully, and the consequences of bullying. You will learn how to stop bullying—whether you are a victim, a bully, or a bystander. You will also learn where to get help.

"I would have done almost anything to make it stop, but I could not figure out how. Every day it felt like I was smaller and weaker than the day before." Ralph, aged 13.

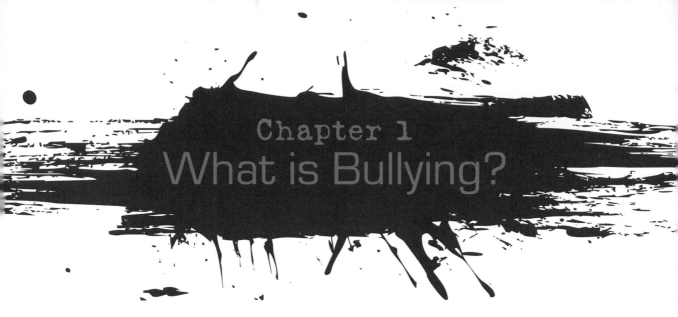

# Chapter 1
# What is Bullying?

Bullying is the act of hurting and **intimidating** another person. Bullying can be physical, such as shoving or hitting. Bullying can also be emotional, such as name-calling. Bullying always involves the abuse of power. Bullying rarely happens once. Instead, it happens repeatedly.

## Bullying = Hurt

Bullies want to hurt other people. Bullies want their victims to feel bad or scared. Bullies would not exist without the desire to hurt another person. Friends can also hurt each other, but usually not on purpose. Bullying is always on purpose.

## Bullying = Intimidation

Intimidation means making someone feel afraid. Bullies intimidate people to make them feel scared and vulnerable. Bullying happens over time. Victims suffer because bullying rarely happens once. It can go on for weeks, months, or even years.

# The Face of Bullying

Bullying can happen anywhere, whether at home, at school, or at work. Adults are sometimes bullied by bosses or spouses. Males and females bully in equal numbers. In the younger grades, boys bully by using more physical **aggression** than girls.

Where does bullying occur? DoSomething.org wanted to know the answer to that question. In April 2012, the organization launched the Bully App on Facebook. By September, more than 185,000 young people responded to the survey. Girls reported seeing bullying mostly online or in the hallways at school. Boys said they saw bullying mostly in the hallways and locker rooms.

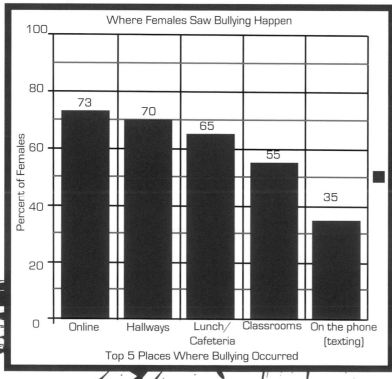

This graph shows the top five places where girls saw bullying taking place.

Source: DoSomething.org

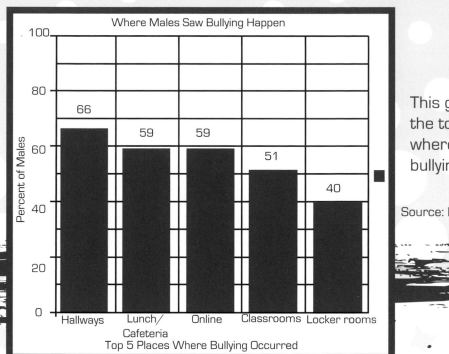

**Where Males Saw Bullying Happen**

Percent of Males

- Hallways: 66
- Lunch/Cafeteria: 59
- Online: 59
- Classrooms: 51
- Locker rooms: 40

Top 5 Places Where Bullying Occurred

This graph shows the top five places where boys saw bullying taking place.

Source: DoSomething.org

Sometimes bullying takes place in groups. Bullying by more than one person often occurs in middle school and high school. During adolescence, young people seek the social acceptance and approval of their peers. **Peer pressure**, and the need to feel accepted, is one reason groups of students bully others.

## Mean Movies

Of course, some bullies have plenty of friends. Yet, they still enjoy harming others. Bullies believe that showing cruelty toward another person earns them respect. This type of bully was featured in the movie *Mean Girls*, starring Lindsay Lohan. In the movie, Lohan plays a student who is accepted by a popular girl **clique**. Her new friends pressure Lohan's character into becoming a mean girl herself.

"Every time she came after me, I wondered what I had done to deserve it. When she took my phone, I didn't even want to go home." Tanya, aged 16.

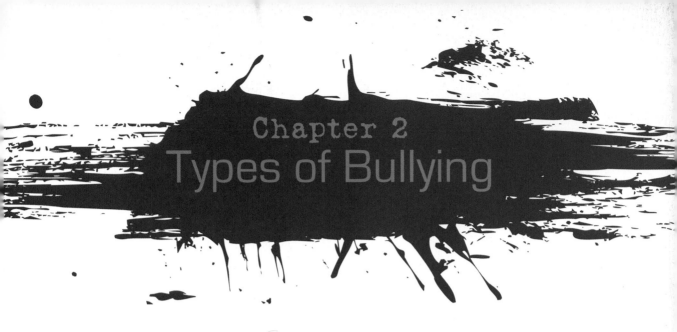

# Chapter 2
# Types of Bullying

There are many kinds of bullying. Bullying can be as simple as quiet whispers in the hall, or finger-pointing in the cafeteria. It can occur in the form of text messages, notes passed in class, or comments written on Facebook or Twitter. The main types of bullying include physical bullying, emotional bullying, and cyber bullying.

## Physical Bullying

Examples of physical bullying include swarming, shoving, hitting, knocking down, choking, or **restraining** a person. The bully may use physical power to mock the victim. For example, before a group of teen bullies beat and drowned 14-year-old Reena Virk in Saanich, British Columbia, a girl put out a cigarette on her forehead. Spitting on someone is another example of using physical power to mock.

Hiding or destroying another person's belongings is a milder form of physical bullying. Physical bullying can lead to injury or even death as it did in Reena Virk's case.

"You experience the same feelings as watching the scary movies everyone else loves but you hate: chills, rapid heartbeat, dry mouth, fear, that sickening pull in your gut. You try again, just to talk to someone. Anyone. But even the people who have no one to talk to—the girl who doesn't wash her hair, the boy who still picks his nose—they won't speak to you." Emily, aged 15.

## Rude Gestures

Rude **gestures** are also a form of physical bullying. A gesture is a kind of non-verbal communication. You can make gestures with your hands, your tongue, or your eyes.

Rude gestures insult or exclude a person. For example, holding up a middle finger in someone's face **degrades** that person. Rolling your eyes at someone is a way of dismissing his or her importance. Even staring can be threatening if it is meant to be upsetting. Refusing to make eye contact with a person who is trying to speak to you is also rude. Although not life-threatening, rude gestures are hurtful and unacceptable.

# Emotional Bullying

Emotional bullying includes saying mean, hurtful things, writing hurtful, **anonymous** letters, calling people names, spreading **rumors**, insulting a person's physical size or appearance, or insulting someone's intelligence.

Emotional bullying does not involve physical injury. However, emotional abuse can hurt a person more than physical abuse.

## By the Numbers

- More than 160,000 students in the United States stay home from school each day out of fear of being bullied.
- Every seven minutes a child is bullied on the playground.
- 43 percent of students fear being harassed in the school bathroom.

Source: stompoutbullying.org

Pointing at or mocking another person is a form of bullying.

13

## Sticks and Stones

No doubt you've heard people hurl insults at a particular individual. Perhaps you have used the same terms yourself. All your friends use those words; why shouldn't you? First, ask yourself if you know what these words really mean. Then ask yourself how you would feel if someone called you those words.

If you see someone calling another person names, tell them to stop. Often having one person stand up to them can make a bully stop picking on someone. If they do not stop, speak to an adult about what you have witnessed.

## Name-calling

"What a moron." "You jerk." "You're a retard." Did you know that name-calling is a form of bullying?

Name-calling can insult a person's **race**, **ethnicity**, religion, or mental or physical abilities.

For example, racial and ethnic insults use negative **stereotypes**. A stereotype is a widely held but oversimplified view or image of a person or group of people. An example of a racial or ethnic stereotype is "all blacks are good athletes." "All Hispanics are illegals" is another stereotype.

The U.S. Department of Health and Human Services says that students with physical disabilities are more likely to be bullied than any other group.

# Rumors and Gossip

"Hey, did you know Jeannie wears her sister's old clothes?"

"Really, her sister's old clothes?"

"Yeah, really. Becky told me that Sarah saw Jeannie at Pizza Villa the other night. Jeannie had the same dress on that her older sister wore at the mall Tuesday. I don't even think it was washed."

"My mom says Jeannie's family doesn't have a lot of money because her father drinks. Plus, their house isn't as big as ours. I think the whole family is trash."

Such conversations are forms of bullying. That's because two people are spreading rumors or repeating **gossip**. Sometimes these activities are innocent. Other times, rumors and gossip cross the line into bullying. The chart below will help you know when you or others are crossing the line.

| It's Innocent When... | It's Bullying When... |
|---|---|
| You repeat information you were told is okay to repeat. | You repeat hurtful gossip as though it were fact. |
| You tell a fake story that is a joke and does not involve real people. | You tell lies about someone. |
| You repeat information that is not damaging to anyone. | You reveal private information about a person that will damage his or her reputation. |

# Sent by "Anonymous"

In Saskatchewan, a province in Canada, a 13-year-old receives an unsigned note in her locker telling her to kill herself. In Leeds, a city in Great Britain, a 14-year-old boy is passed a note that says, "Adam's got big ears and if they get any bigger they will fly." In Maryland, someone **vandalizes** a girl's locker using a sanitary pad.

No one knows who sent the letters or did the vandalizing. Yet, such anonymous communication is a form of bullying. In fact, anonymous communication is a common way to bully others. Bullies can torment their victims without worrying about getting caught.

For the victim, however, such unsigned communication makes the situation worse. Everyone is a suspect. It makes it difficult to trust anyone. It makes it hard to relax among friends.

Sending anonymous notes and making anonymous calls have become more common in recent years because of the Internet and wireless communication. This form of bullying is called cyber bullying.

Texting is a new way for bullies to target people.

16

# Cyber Bullying

A cyber bully uses a device, such as a computer or a mobile phone, to send harmful or threatening messages to another person. The cyber bully can also intimidate the victim in a chat room or through text messaging. He or she can spread rumors about someone through email or postings on a social media site.

Technology gives cyber bullies the power to reach a wide audience. In most cases, cyber bullying takes place anonymously.

Sometimes cyber bullies **impersonate** others. In this situation, the bully pretends to be someone else. Consider what happened in 2006 to Megan Meier. Megan struck up a MySpace conversation with a 16-year-old boy she thought was named "Josh Evans."

The two became good online friends. Megan was thrilled to have the attention of a boy. By the fall of 2006, the tone of Josh's messages changed. He accused her of being nasty to her friends. His last words to her were, "The world would be a better place without you."

Megan read those words and killed herself three weeks before she turned 14. Police later learned that the "Josh Evans" MySpace account had been created by an adult—the mother of one of Megan's friends. The mother set up the account to torment Megan because Megan had **allegedly** spread rumors about her daughter.

"I don't really want to, and I know it's wrong, but I get some kind of joy out of making fun of others and gossiping about them. I also like to pretend to be other people to see what people say about me or to see how they will react to some mean things I can say about the person I am pretending to be." Richard, aged 16.

# Chapter 3
# The Bully

Bullies crave power. They use it to hurt others. Why does a bully become a bully? Over the years, psychologists have focused their attention on four reasons.

## Short Fuse

According to certain studies, bullies are quicker to anger than most people. Sometimes they have a hard time controlling their emotions. Bullies often become angry if they are insulted or offended. They do not like when others cause them to think badly about themselves. As a result, bullies lash out. A bully may have negative **role models**. He or she might have family members who are also quick to lose their tempers or who are violent.

One thing is certain. Bullies are hooked on bullying. They enjoy the attention they receive from their actions. Bullies believe that by harming others, their **social status** will be enhanced. Moreover, bullies feel so good when they threaten, intimidate, and harass that it is hard for them to stop.

# Can't Relate

Bullies don't care about the feelings of their victims. They enjoy watching others suffer. Such reactions are the result of low **empathy**. Empathy means imagining yourself in another person's situation to understand what that person is feeling.

Empathy develops over time. For example, when you were a small child, you might have grabbed another child's toy because you liked it. In order to teach you empathy, your parent or teacher might have asked, "How would you like it if Sarah took your toy?" Gradually, you learned to consider the other person's feelings.

Bullies may not lack empathy, but refuse to show any. They are more concerned with being liked and admired by others. They may have decided that thinking about another person's feelings is something that they should not worry about.

## By the Numbers

According to the National Education Association:
- 33 percent of all students in grades six through ten said they were affected by bullying.
- 83 percent of girls and 79 percent of boys report being harassed at school.

Source: National Education Association

## Nice Bullies?

Everyone has heard of the nice kids who for some reason became bullies. How did it happen? Why did it happen? Like all bullies, even nice bullies want social approval. Bullies work hard to get other people to bully with them. Bullies might insist that the victim deserves it. Those who join in the bullying feel important, too. Once several people are involved in bullying, it is hard for anyone to withdraw or disagree.

## Family Affair

Bullies often come from **dysfunctional** families where discipline is inconsistent. The bully might also be abused physically, mentally, or sexually by family members. As a result, the bully feels a sense of powerlessness. In turn, they bully other children to regain a sense of control over their lives.

Bullies like to torment others in groups.

"One day I saw this girl get bullied just because she was a little bit different than everyone else. They were calling her "stupid" and other things, too. I felt really bad for her. I didn't do anything really, I just talked to the girl about it and I told her that I understood." Shanice, aged 16.

# Chapter 4
## The Victim

Phoebe Prince had just moved from Ireland to South Hadley, Massachusetts when she began dating a popular football player at South Hadley High. Phoebe was only 15 at the time, and a freshman, the lowest of the low in high school. Some of her classmates did not approve of the relationship.

In response, they wrote awful comments about Phoebe on Facebook. They started rumors. They insulted her. They sent Phoebe cruel text messages. The bullying went on for three months.

On January 14, 2010, Phoebe committed suicide. Several weeks later, a state **prosecutor** filed criminal charges against several of Phoebe's classmates saying they had engaged in "relentless activities" that made it impossible for Phoebe to stay in school.

Phoebe Prince was a bullying victim. Although the victims of bullying are a diverse group, they share certain characteristics.

# Picking Their Victim

Bullies carefully pick their victims. Some bullies target smaller kids who cannot defend themselves. Bullies crave admiration and approval and will target those that others will not defend. Victims, such as Phoebe Prince, might be new to a school. They might be shy or quieter than other students. Some are just different.

People are different because they have unique characteristics, interests and abilities. They usually stand out in some way. Bullies pick on people who stand out. Bullies have a need for control. They want to decide who fits in. Bullies may pick on racial minorities, or people who are lesbian, gay, bisexual, or **transgendered** (LGBT).

Bullying victims suffer from self-esteem issues, depression, and other mental disorders. In many instances, victims can become violent, or like Phoebe, suicidal.

## By the Numbers

A survey of middle and high school students by the Centers for Disease Control and Prevention shows that eight out of ten LGBT students had been verbally bullied at school and four out of ten had been physically bullied.

Source: Centers for Disease Control and Prevention

Bullies will target homosexuals more than heterosexual adolescents.

## Payback Time

Some bullies may believe that the victims are the source of their problems. The bullies might believe that victims stole their boyfriends or girlfriends, or spread rumors about them. In some cases, the bullies might be right. In these situations, bullies are seeking revenge. They want the victims to feel as embarrassed and hurt as they do.

The desire to hurt someone who hurt you is a powerful emotion. Bullies have a hard time letting go of these negative feelings.

"When I was in fourth grade, it was the first time I ever got bullied. A girl came up to me and just said, 'You're stupid and ugly. You don't even belong at this school.' That's where it all began.

In fifth grade, the girls would call me ugly and stupid for piling on tons of makeup. Sometimes they would call me fat.

"I've been called emo and goth because of the music I listen to and the way that I sometimes dress. I'm going to tell an adult the next time I'm bullied." Kendra, aged 12.

"There she was sitting in the parking lot. She was crying. Off in the distance the others were laughing at her. I had seen her in the hall before as they taunted her. I wanted to go to her and say the other kids were jerks, and that she shouldn't let it get her down. I didn't go. I didn't say a word to her." Tony, aged 14.

# Chapter 5
## The Bystander

Have you ever seen someone being bullied? Did you try to help? Chances are you didn't. You might have felt that if you tried to **intervene**, the bully would come after you. You were a bystander. A bystander is person who watches while an event—often a crime—takes place but does nothing to stop it.

According to The Bully Report published by DoSomething.org, 76 percent of teens want other students to get involved when they see a bullying incident. However, only 16 percent say students try to stop bullying at their school.

Why don't some people help? For one thing, some students don't want to be known as a "rat." In other words, they don't want to be called a tattletale. Others believe that if they report their friends as bullies, they will become less popular.

Bystanders worry about becoming victims themselves. Also, bystanders may not realize the impact they can have. Many don't realize that more than half of the time bullying stops within ten seconds when someone helps.

# Bystander Effect

The **bystander effect** occurs when several people see a bad event and do nothing to stop it. The larger the group, the less likely individuals will think there is a problem, and therefore, the less likely it will be that they will take action.

There are two reasons for this reaction, says psychologist Sam Sommers. First, when we're in a group, each of us believes that someone else will take care of the problem.

Second, when we are unsure about what an event means, we tend to observe the reactions of other people. "When no one else seems alarmed, we're more likely to keep to ourselves as well," says Sommers.

# Crowd Control

It's sometimes hard to stop a bully when you're part of a crowd. When a person is part of a group, it influences their behavior. We no longer think about our own actions. We also wonder what other people will do. We wonder what they will think of us if we say, or do, something different. It takes courage to stand up in a crowd.

Students who witness nonstop bullying often feel powerless.

# The Bullying Circle

Bullying is a vicious cycle. A Norwegian researcher named Dan Olweus developed a special model to explain how the cycle works. The model is called the Bullying Circle. The circle shows what different kinds of bystanders think when confronted by an episode of bullying.

As you can see, most bystanders do not support the bullying. However, their silence means that the bullying continues.

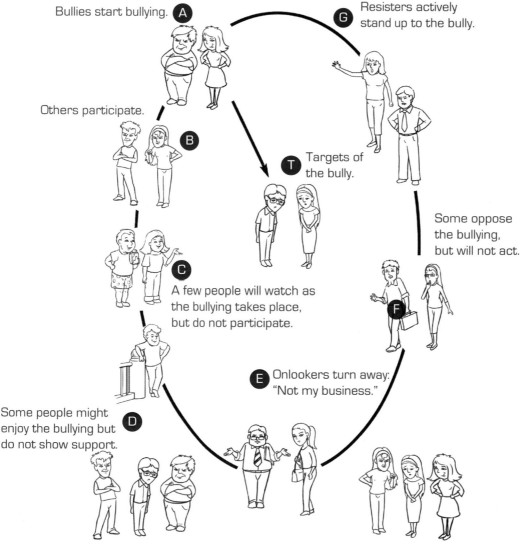

Bullies start bullying. **A**

Resisters actively stand up to the bully. **G**

Others participate. **B**

Targets of the bully. **T**

Some oppose the bullying, but will not act.

A few people will watch as the bullying takes place, but do not participate. **C**

Some people might enjoy the bullying but do not show support. **D**

Onlookers turn away: "Not my business." **E**

**F**

"Every day I woke up with a stomachache. Every day my parents told me it would get better and to stand up for myself. It did not get better. It got worse."
Jada, aged 17.

# Chapter 6
# Consequences

Felicia Garcia was a bullied teenager. The 15-year-old Staten Island, New York, high school freshmen had heard the vicious rumors. Everyone said that she had had sex with a group of guys from the Tottenville high school football team.

"They wouldn't leave her alone about it," one of Felicia's friends told the *New York Daily News*. "They just kept bullying her and bullying her."

The bullying ended when Felicia jumped onto a railroad track and committed suicide. "I cant, im done, I give up," she posted on Twitter just before an oncoming train struck and killed her.

On Felicia's Instagram account she posted a shout out for help. She had placed a picture of herself with the word "depressed" over the photo. "Just because someone is smiling doesn't make them happy," she had written.

# Victimized

Bullying has consequences not only for the victim, but everyone involved, including bullies and bystanders. Ken Rigby, a bullying expert from Australia, says there are three ways in which victims suffer from bullying.

First, bullying can cause a victim to fear others. As a result, victims might not socialize or make new friends. They avoid going to school. They miss work. They do not do well on assignments and tests.

Second, like Felicia or Phoebe Prince, victims of bullying often feel depressed and anxious. That's because they live in fear. Victims do not know when they will be attacked again. They feel lonely. Bullying can cause many physical problems, including headaches, stomachaches, and sleeping problems.

Lastly, a study by the Cyberbullying Research Center found that the victims of cyber bullying are twice as likely to have attempted suicide compared to those who had not been victims of cyber bullying.

Bullies can push a person to harm themselves.

# Bully, Bully

Tim Hutchinson taught at a college where his boss bullied him. The boss made fun of Hutchinson's accent and verbally attacked him in meetings. He told the staff that Hutchinson was a poor teacher. Hutchinson became so upset that he left the school and quit teaching.

What happens when bullies grow up? It's simple. They generally become adult bullies. These individuals have poor relationships because of their need for power and control. When they were young, they did not learn the importance of empathy and respect. As a result, they entered adulthood with little chance of having warm, respectful relationships.

Dan Olweus, who created the Bullying Circle, looked at what happened to bullies when they got older. He found some went on to become criminals. In fact, 60 percent of boys that teachers labeled as bullies in grades six through nine had committed at least one crime by the time they turned 24. Another study found that 27 percent of girls who were bullied later became bullies themselves.

"The bullying in our school had gone on long enough.
It was time to do something. Janice and I went to
Ms. Vickers and asked what we could do. We formed
a committee to help stop bullying." Ashley, aged 16.

# Chapter 7
# Stop the Bullying

You have learned what bullying is, where it occurs, why people bully, and the different forms bullying takes. You know about victims, bullies, and bystanders. Now it is time to take action and learn now to prevent bullying.

If you are the victim of a bully, your first step is to learn what you can do. You can speak to the bully. Stay calm and be direct. Say to him or her: "I don't like what you're doing," or "leave me alone." Do not insult the bully—that will make things worse. Walk away when you are finished speaking. If you feel afraid, bring a friend with you.

If you are unsure about speaking to the bully, try to avoid places where he or she is going to be. Ask a friend to walk to school with you, or join a group of students at recess.

# Report the Bully

Whether you speak to a bully or not, you should report the bullying. Talk to a family member, teacher, principal, or guidance counselor. When you report bullying, be as specific as possible. Being specific means giving details that will help the other person understand.

If you do not want to report the bully in person, you can file a bully report. Canadians can file such a report by going to StopABully.ca. In the United States, you can search the Internet with the key terms *bully report* + *your location*. Many school districts offer this option. When you complete your report, it will be sent to your principal. Experts recommend filling out the report with an adult.

If you are being bullied at school, tell an older sibling, teacher, a counselor, or the principal.

# Look After Yourself

It is never fun to be bullied. Talk to someone about how you feel. If you are depressed, speak to a family member or a school counselor. Tell them how long you have been bullied. Use words that describe your emotions such as: "I feel like locking myself in my room and never coming out," or "being at school feels like being in a horror movie."

If bullying has been ongoing, your family might consider transferring you to another school. Moving doesn't address the root of the problem, but it might be necessary if you are in danger. However, this is a decision that you, your family, and school staff should make together. If your family is uncertain, speak to a teacher first and ask that person to speak to your parent or guardian.

Tell someone immediately if you feel suicidal. Suicidal feelings should always be taken seriously. Counseling can help you feel better. You can call the National Suicide Prevention Hotline in the United States or Canada.

Bullying doesn't have to be a locked door. There are many things that you can do to stop bullying.

# Battling the Cyber Bully

Here are some steps you can take to protect your safety if you are the victim of a cyber bully:

- Never reply to cyber bullies, but do not delete any of their messages. Save emails, chats, text messages, and photos. Save screen captures of Web sites and social media pages. Print as much of the material as you can.
- Report cyber bullies to your family. Your parent or guardian will understand that you are the victim of bullying. Don't keep silent because you are afraid of losing your phone or Internet privileges.
- Use Internet reporting systems to report the cyber bullies. Look for a Web site button that says "Report Abuse" and follow the instructions.
- Block the sender on social networking sites. Find the block command under headings such as Tools or Privacy.
- With an adult, report cyber bullies to the police if the messages become threatening.
- Report cyber bullies the way you would report any bully by using the bully report.

- Log out of your accounts completely when you leave a computer. Do not save passwords on the computer, especially a public computer.
- Never share your password with anyone except your family members.
- Avoid posting details about yourself. Do not give out your personal information. Do not post multiple pictures of yourself. Do not get into arguments online. Remember, your words can survive for a long time on the Internet.
- Search for your name once a month. If you see personal information that does not belong there, try to get it removed.

Log out completely when using shared computers. This keeps your information safe.

# If You Are Bullying

If you are a bully, ask yourself why? What are you getting out of it? Are you looking for attention? Are you looking to be popular? If so, there are other ways to achieve your goal.

Find a hobby or a sport that can occupy your time and take you away from bullying. Talk to someone, such as a counselor or teacher. Asking for help is a sign of maturity—no one will shame you for asking.

You might need help with empathy and anger management. Counselors can help teach you these skills. Check with the guidance department at your school or phone the Kids Help Phone Line (see page 47). The service is anonymous and free.

Remember that bullying has negative consequences for you, too. You could be expelled from school or you could be arrested. If you act like a bully when you're a kid, you will more than likely act like a bully as an adult. Personal and work relationships will be difficult to maintain.

# Say You're Sorry

Consider apologizing to your victims. You might think that an apology will not mean much, but it usually does. Victims of bullies who receive an apology say it helps them heal and put the past behind. One victim heard from a bully years later. She said it was a miracle that gave her hope.

If you feel awkward apologizing in person, write a note. In order for your apology to be sincere, you should:

- Admit that you hurt the person.
  - Say you are sorry for causing pain in their life.
    - Explain that you are working to stop your actions because you know it is destructive.

You do not have to be friends with your victims. You simply need to acknowledge your actions and show that you mean to change.

A sincere apology will help both the bully and the victim move on.

# If You Are a Bystander

If you see bullying in your school, remember the bystander effect. When bullying starts, most people do not want it to continue. But research shows that when bystanders intervene, there is a 50 percent chance that the bullying will stop.

How do you stop someone from bullying another person? Place yourself between the victim and the bully. Look at the bully and say, "You should stop doing that," or "Why don't you walk away?" Offer to walk the victim out of the area.

If you do not speak up, the bully will assume that everyone approves of his or her actions. If you are with a friend, encourage that person to speak up, too. Act quickly— as soon as the bullying starts. When bystanders wait, it becomes harder to intervene.

Speaking up and being supportive of one another can help end bullying.

# Getting Your School Involved

Does your school have an anti-bullying program? An anti-bullying program is a way many schools respond to bullying. It supports students and teachers in raising bullying awareness. Anti-bullying programs support students by providing them with :

- information to help students understand and stop bullying;

- an anti-bully committee that meets to discuss ways to reduce bullying;

- classroom opportunities so students can express their feelings about bullying;

- special events such as STAND UP to Bullying Day.

If your school does not have such a program, speak to your principal about starting one. Try to identify teachers who would be willing to sit on an anti-bullying committee with students.

If your school already has such a program, get involved with it. Offer to help students who have a bullying problem. Publicize the school's anti-bullying policy by designing flyers or posters that show how to intervene. Write about STAND UP to Bullying Day in the school newspaper.

## Bullying has always existed. Can anyone really do anything about it?

A: Bullying has always been around, but it has to stop. Recently, many adults have begun to see bullying as a major problem for kids. One way to prevent bullying is with an anti-bullying program at your school or in your community. If there is no program, start one with your principal or another adult. Anti-bullying programs work best when everyone is involved, especially students.

## It seems like I always get bullied in the hallway when nobody is there to help. What can I do?

A: The first thing you should do is tell a trusted adult. Ask another student to walk with you to class or to recess. If your locker is in an isolated area, ask for it to be moved so that the bully cannot corner you.

**I have sent more than 50 mean texts to someone. This person stole my best friend last year. Why should I stop?**

A: It is against the law in many communities to communicate with others repeatedly in order to harm or embarrass them. The victim may be saving your texts or have notified the police. Revenge will not make you feel better. Talk about your feelings with someone you trust. Finally, apologize to the person you harassed.

**Being the reject sucks. I spend a lot of time in my bedroom alone and upset. Nobody notices me. Will anything change?**

A: Feeling alone and upset is hard, especially when you are a preteen or teen. Miranda Jones (not her real name) was teased about her weight in high school and upset all the time. One day, she decided to join the debate team. She said the activity kept her busy. She also discovered she was good at it. She made some wonderful friends. Try to find an activity you love that will put you in touch with people who share your interests. Friendship often starts with common interests.

**I cannot think of anyone to talk to. Maybe I should just give up.**

A: You can talk to any trusted adult. It does not have to be a family member or a teacher. It could be a coach or a neighbor. You could also phone the Kids Help Phone. You can get information and counseling about bullying.

The following Web sites will provide you with trustworthy information about bullying.

## In the United States

### Kids Against Bullying
http://www.pacerkidsagainstbullying.org/#/home
An interactive Web site created by and for kids to raise awareness of bullying in elementary school.

### Stop Bullying
http://www.stopbullying.gov/
This Web site brings together the expertise of many U.S. agencies on how to explain and prevent bullying. Check out how not to be a bystander.

### It's My Life
http://pbskids.org/itsmylife/friends/bullies/
A lot of information about bullies, gossip, and rumors, as well as the emotional roller coaster of adolescence.

# In Canada

Bullying.org

http://www.bullying.org/

Information for kids and adults on preventing bullying through awareness and education.

## Bullying Awareness Week

This site publicizes Bullying Awareness Week in November and features many student-made videos.

## Stop a Bully

http://www.stopabully.ca/

The way to safely and anonymously report a bully to your school.

# Hotlines

## Kids Help Phone

www.kidshelpphone.ca

1-800-668-6868

Support forums for teens will help you see that you are not alone. Anonymous, confidential counseling is also available online. Phone counseling is available only to callers in Canada.

## National Suicide Prevention Lifeline

http://www.suicidepreventionlifeline.org/

1-800-273-TALK

Support for those who are emotionally distressed or suicidal.

## The BRAVE Campaign Hotline (U.S. only)

(212-709-3222, M-F 2:30-9:30 p.m.)

Afterschool anti-bullying hotline run by the United Federation of Teachers. Students can find out who could be an ally in their school.

# Glossary

**aggression** Hostile or destructive behavior

**allegedly** Believed to be without proof

**anonymous** Describes someone with no name or identity

**bystander effect** The tendency for a group of people to resist helping someone in need

**clique** A small group of people that spend time together while excluding others

**degrades** Disgraces; humiliates

**dysfunctional** Not working properly

**empathy** Understanding another's feelings

**ethnicity** A group with a common culture, nationality and background

**gestures** Non-verbal communication with your body

**gossip** Stories or rumors of an intimate nature

**intervene** To come between two people in order to stop their interaction

**intimidating** Frightening someone into doing what you want

**peer pressure** Pressure from friends and acquaintances to behave in a certain way

**prosecutor** An attorney who represents the government in a criminal trial

**race** Human groups

**restraining** Forcibly holding down

**role model** People others look up to because of their behavior and outlook

**rumors** Stories that have not been confirmed and may be false

**social status** Position in a social hierarchy

**stereotypes** Images of groups of people that are over-simplified and untrue

**transgendered** Relating to a person who does not identify with the sexuality to which they were born

**vandalizes** Destroys or defaces property

# Index